Lettering Through Lent

PRAYERS, HYMNS, SCRIPTURE, & SAINTS

Lorelei Worland
BOOKS FAITH LIFE

About the Author

Lorelei has designed and sold beautiful goods through her store, Books Faith Life Shop, since 2017.

This is her third book in a series of handlettering guides.

Lorelei lives with her husband, son, and lazy dachshund on the sunny Mississippi gulf coast.

You can find more about her and her work at booksfaithlife.com

Anatomy of a Letter

1. Baseline

The line where all letters rest. Shown in dark grey.

2. Meanline

The midline where lowercase letters without ascenders terminate. Shown in light grey.

3. Cap line

The line where uppercase letters terminate. Shown in dark grey.

Anatomy of a Letter

4. Ascender

The part of the letter that goes above the midline.

5. Descender

The part of the letter that dips below the baseline.

6. Upstroke

The upward stroke of the letter. By **decreasing** pressure on your soft-tip brush pen, the upstroke becomes the thinnest part of the letter.

7. Downstroke

The downward stroke of the letter. By **increasing** gentle pressure on your soft-tip brush pen, the downstroke becomes the thickest part of the letter.

Ff Gg Mm Qq

Supplies needed:

1. Brush pen

You will need a **soft-tip** brush pen to create the thick & thin lines characteristic of modern hand lettering. This is the only must-have writing implement for this workbook.

My favorite brush pens are the Tombow™ Fudenosuke Soft Tips. They're smooth and flexible enough to finish this workbook with ease.

You can buy individual pens from craft stores for around $3.

2. Scratch paper

While you have lots of space for practice, I like to warm up my letterforms on scratch paper first. A smooth, premium printer paper is the most economical choice. Or for the best effect, use a marker or watercolor paper.

Let's Get Started

Thank you for choosing this book as your Lenten companion. Each day you'll open to the next assignment, and a new quote to practice lettering.

Each Sunday's quote comes from the Introit, or entrance antiphon, of the Mass. The other quotes come from scripture, Saints, and classic hymns

You can also color in the decorative wreaths, borders, and bouquets. The quote pages are single sided, so you can cut them out and display your work..

Finally, you can download extra practice pages and beautiful full-color Easter pages at www.booksfaithlife.com/easter

Go slowly. Practice often. Most of all, have fun!

In Christ,

Lorelei Worland

Ash Wednesday

Under Pressure

As we learned in the introduction, the defining look of brush lettering is one of thick downstrokes and slender upstrokes.

Random, variable stroke thickness looks unbalanced.

The theory is straightforward. When your pen is moving downward, exert a steady, slight pressure. This brings the thicker portion of your pen nib down to the paper. The result is a wider line.

Whenever your pen moves horizontally (like crossing a t), or moves upward, release the pressure. These low-pressure strokes use just the narrow tip of your pen nib, creating a graceful line.

Getting consistent strokes with smooth transitions takes time and effort. There's no substitute for practice.

Begin releasing pressure before the transition. Your pen nib needs time to spring back.

Gently release pressure before the curve to flow into a narrow upstroke. This will narrow the thick line into a triangle at the bottom of the downstroke,

Pay close attention to the direction of your pen's movement when choosing pressure.

Be sure to practice your strokes (up, down, horizontal, diagonal, and circles) on scratch paper. You are training the muscles in your hand, wrist, and arm. With practice, you will create consistent pressure for steady lines and transitions.

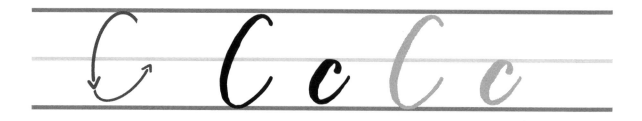

Aa

A A A A A A

A A A A A A

a a a a a a a

a a a a a a a

Ash

Aa

A A A A A

A A A A A

a a a a a a a

a a a a a a a

Ash

Your mercy extends to all things. O Lord.

Bb

B B B B B

B B B B B

b b b b b b

b b b b b b

Behold

Bb

B B B B B

B B B B B

b b b b b b b

b b b b b b b

Behold

His mercies are new
every morning.

Cc

C C C C C

C C C C C

c c c c c c c

c c c c c c c

Come

Cc

C C C C C

C C C C C

c c c c c c c

c c c c c c c

Come

God's mercy is stronger
than our misery.
St. Faustina

Dd

D D D D D D

D D D D D D

d d d d d d

d d d d d d

Deliver

Dd

D D D D D D

D D D D D D

d d d d d d

d d d d d d

Deliver

Streams of mercy,
never ceasing, call for
songs of loudest praise.

The First Sunday

Take a Break

When we learned cursive in school, we were told to not take our pencil off the page. Handlettering is more like painting than cursive though. You need to take your brush off the page frequently.

These pauses allow you to adjust pressure, evaluate your progress, and make corrections going forward.

Your pen might leave the page before every downstroke, between each letter, or even more often. Do what feels and looks right to you.

Don't worry about finishing quickly. Your speed will improve with practice. Even experienced letterers take it slow, and letter more slowly than writing in manuscript.

This week, be sure to let your pen leave the page as often as necessary to reposition, evaluate, and reset your pressure.

Ee

E E E E E

E E E E E

e e e e e

e e e e e

Enter

Ee

E E E E E

E E E E E

e e e e e

e e e e e

Enter

He will call upon me, and I will answer Him.

Ff

F F F F F

F F F F F

f f f f f

f f f f f

Faith

Ff

F F F F F

F F F F F

f f f f f

f f f f f

Faith

Teach us, Good Lord, to
serve You as You deserve.
St. Ignatius

Gg

G G G G G G

G G G G G G

g g g g g g

g g g g g g

Grace

Gg

G G G G G G

G G G G G G

g g g g g

g g g g g

Grace

I desire to do your will.
my God: your law is
within my heart.

Psalm 40:8

Hh

H H H H H

H H H H H

h h h h h

h h h h h

Help

Hh

H H H H H

H H H H H

h h h h h

h h h h h

Help

Take my life, and let it be
consecrated, Lord, to
Thee.

Ii

I I I I I

I I I I I

i i i i i

i i i i i

Imagine

Ii

I I I I I

I I I I I

i i i i i

i i i i i

Imagine

I want to do God's
Holy Will, not my own!

St. Gabriel of
the Sorrowful Mother

Jj

J J J J J J

J J J J J J

j j j j j j

j j j j j j

Jesus

Jj

J J J J J J

J J J J J J

j j j j j j

j j j j j j

Jesus

For the LORD Almighty has purposed, and who can thwart him?

Isaiah 14:27

Kk

K K K K K

K K K K K

k k k k k

k k k k k

King

Kk

K K K K K

K K K K K

k k k k k

k k k k k

King

Speak, O Lord, Your
servant listens, let Your
Word to me come near.

The Second
Sunday

Curves Ahead

This week we're going to focus on circular shapes.

Since this week includes the letters O, P, Q and R, it's a great opportunity to study the challenges of clockwise vs. counterclockwise motions.

For once your strokes here are not limited by habit, but by anatomy.

Right-handed letterers make smooth, fluid counterclockwise circles. But clockwise motions are difficult. Why? Because they stretch the wrist to the limit of its range of motion.

Left-handed letterers experience the opposite. A clockwise circle is easy and open. Whereas the spontaneous counterclockwise circle is sharp and angular.

Give your wrists a break!

Before a challenging circle, lift up your pen and begin a new starting point.

A challenging circle direction should always begin with a new stroke. Don't throw it in as an afterthought.

Clockwise	Counterclockwise
Bb *D* *Pp* *R*	*Aa* *Cc* *d* *e* *f* *Gg* *Oo* *Qq* *Uu* *Yy*

L l

L L L L L

L L L L L

l l l l l

l l l l l

Love

L l

L L L L L

L L L L L

l l l l l

l l l l l

Love

My heart says of you, "Seek His face!" Your face, Lord, I will seek.

M m

M M M M M M M M M M

M M M M M M M M M M

m m m m m m m m m m

m m m m m m m m m m

Mary

M m

M M M M M

M M M M M

m m m m m

m m m m m

Mary

God gives Himself to those who give up all for Him.

St. Teresa of Avila

Nn

N N N N N

N N N N N

n n n n n

n n n n n

Nurture

N n

N N N N N

N N N N N

n n n n n

n n n n n

Nurture

For the Son of Man came
to seek and to save the lost.

Luke 19:10

Oo

O O O O O

O O O O O

O O O O O

O O O O O

Our Lady

Oo

O O O O O

O O O O O

O o o o o

O o o o o

Our Lady

Be thou my vision.
O Lord of my heart.

Pp

p p p p p p

p p p p p p

p p p p p p

p p p p p p

Peace

Pp

p p p p p p

p p p p p p

p p p p p p

p p p p p p

Peace

The greater one's love,
the easier the work.
St. Augustine

Qq

Q Q Q Q Q

Q Q Q Q Q

q q q q q

q q q q q

Quiet

Qq

Q Q Q Q Q

Q Q Q Q Q

q q q q q

q q q q q

Quiet

Rr

R R R R R

R R R R R

r r r r r

r r r r r

Restore

R r

R R R R R

R R R R R

r r r r r

r r r r r

Restore

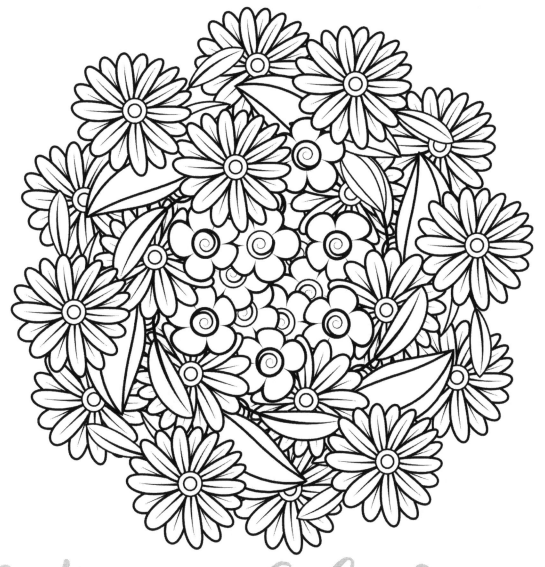

Restore us, O God; make
your face shine on us,
that we may be saved.
Psalm 80:3

The Third Sunday

Pressure Transitions

This week tests your pressure transitions like none other.

Remember: pressure changes the thickness of lines. Downward strokes are heavier and thick. Upward strokes are lighter and thin.

Begin releasing pressure before the transition. Your pen nib needs time to spring back. Gently release pressure before the curve to flow into a narrow upstroke. This will narrow the thick line into a triangle.

Reverse the process to transition from upstroke to downstrokes. Increase pressure just before the switch. You want to see a beautiful triangle appear each time.

Ss Tt Uu Vv Ww Xx Yy

A note on nibs:

A frayed or misshapen nib will mess up all your hard work.

You needn't push too hard. Yes, the base of the pen must be in contact with the paper to form thick downstrokes. To preserve the quality of the nib, you want to use the least force necessary. Experiment on scratch paper to find the correct pressure.

Always use smooth paper with your brush pen. A premium printer paper is the most economical choice. Or for the best effect, use marker paper or watercolor paper.

Ss

S S S S S

S S S S S

s s s s s

s s s s s

Savior

Ss

$S \quad S \quad S \quad S \quad S$

$S \quad S \quad S \quad S \quad S$

$s \quad s \quad s \quad s \quad s$

$s \quad s \quad s \quad s \quad s$

Savior

My eyes are ever on the LORD, for only he will release my feet from the snare.

Tt

T T T T T

T T T T T

t t t t t

t t t t t

Trust

Tt

T T T T T T

T T T T T T

t t t t t t

t t t t t t

Trust

Hold your eyes on
God and leave the
doing to Him.

St. Jane Frances de Chantal

Uu

U U U U U

U U U U U

u u u u u

u u u u u

Unity

Uu

U U U U U

U U U U U

u u u u u

u u u u u

Unity

His eye is on the
sparrow, and I know he
watches me.

Vv

V V V V V V

V V V V V V

v v v v v v

v v v v v v

Virtue

V v

V V V V V

V V V V V

v v v v v

v v v v v

Virtue

The Lord will rescue his servants; no one who takes refuge in him will be condemned.

Psalm 34:22

Ww

W W W W W

W W W W W

W W W W W

W W W W W

Wisdom

Ww

W W W W W

W W W W W

W W W W W

W W W W W

Wisdom

Humility is
the mother of
many virtues.

St. Thomas of Villanova

Xx

X X X X X

X X X X X

x x x x x

x x x x x

Crucifix

Xx

X X X X X

X X X X X

x x x x x

x x x x x

Crucifix

Be thou my vision, O
Lord of my heart.

Yy

Y Y Y Y Y Y

Y Y Y Y Y Y

y y y y y y

y y y y y y

Yearn

Yy

Y Y Y Y Y Y

Y Y Y Y Y Y

y y y y y y

y y y y y y

Yearn

Fear of man will prove
to be a snare,
but whoever trusts in
the LORD is kept safe.
Proverbs 29:25

The Fourth Sunday

A-Z Was Easy

As we talked about in the second week of Lent, some handlettering challenges come from anatomy, not habit.

O is a wide letter, covering the horizontal reach of your wrist. If you rush straight to the next letter, it will end up narrow. You've run out of wrist range.

Raise and reposition your wrist to keep the next letter from narrowing.

This week, you will finish practicing the alphabet and move onto challenging letter combinations.

Z oa ou ow oi oy ea

Zz

Z Z Z Z Z

Z Z Z Z Z

z z z z z

z z z z z

Zion

Zz

Z Z Z Z Z

Z Z Z Z Z

z z z z z

z z z z z

Zion

oa

oa oa oa oa oa

oa oa oa oa oa

oa oa oa

oa oa oa

Road

oa

oa oa oa oa oa

oa oa oa oa oa

oa oa oa

oa oa oa

Road

At the evening of life,
we shall be judged
on our love.

St. John of the Cross

ou

ou ou ou ou ou

ou ou ou ou ou

ou ou ou

ou ou ou

Fount

ou

ou *ou* *ou* *ou* *ou*

ou *ou* *ou* *ou* *ou*

ou *ou* *ou*

ou *ou* *ou*

Fount

The LORD makes firm the
steps of the one who delights
in Him.
Psalm 37:23

ow

ow ow ow ow ow

ow ow ow ow ow

ow ow ow

ow ow ow

Flower

ow

ow ow ow ow ow

ow ow ow ow ow

ow ow ow

ow ow ow

Flower

oi

oi oi oi oi oi

oi oi oi oi oi

oi oi oi

oi oi oi

Rejoice

oi

oi oi oi oi oi

oi oi oi oi oi

oi oi oi

oi oi oi

Rejoice

I will be glad and rejoice in you: I will sing the praises of your name, O Most High.

Psalm 9:2

oy

oy oy oy oy oy

oy oy oy oy oy

oy oy oy

oy oy oy

Joy

oy

oy oy oy oy oy

oy oy oy oy oy

oy oy oy

oy oy oy

Joy

Joyful, joyful, we adore
Thee, God of glory,
Lord of love.

ea

ea *ea* *ea* *ea* *ea*

ea *ea* *ea* *ea* *ea*

ea *ea* *ea*

ea *ea* *ea*

Peace

ea

ea *ea* *ea* *ea* *ea*

ea *ea* *ea* *ea* *ea*

ea *ea* *ea*

ea *ea* *ea*

Peace

Joy, with peace, is the
sister of charity.

St. Padre Pio

The Fifth Sunday

Common wide letters

Last week we reacted to a wide letter; this week we anticipate them.

Both o and e require a full range of motion from your wrist. They look similar, so you must differentiate the two in your lettering. A clear distinction between your heavier downstrokes and lighter upstrokes is vital.

Pick up your brush pen before ending a word with e. Anticipate this important letter. Reposition your wrist to keep the e from narrowing.

br oe we ve ee oo wr

A sloppy **e** looks like a flourish

The letter **e** is one of the more common word endings in English. Hiding it through lack of planning can change the meaning of a whole sentence. Consider:

breathe

vs

breathe

br

br br br br br

br br br br br

br br br

br br br

Timbrel

br

br br br br br

br br br br br

br br br

br br br

Timbrel

Vindicate me, my God, and plead my cause against an unfaithful nation.

oe

oe oe oe oe oe

oe oe oe oe oe

oe oe oe

oe oe oe

Doe

oe

oe *oe oe oe oe*

oe *oe oe oe oe*

oe *oe oe*

oe *oe oe*

Doe

The gifts of grace
increase as the
struggles increase.

St. Rose of Lima

we

we we we we we

we we we we we

we we we

we we we

Clwe

we

we we we we we

we we we we we

we we we

we we we

Awe

The LORD foils the plans of
the nations; he thwarts the
purposes of the peoples.
Psalm 33:10

ve

ve ve ve ve ve

ve ve ve ve ve

ve ve ve

ve ve ve

Love

ve

ve ve ve ve ve

ve ve ve ve ve

ve ve ve

ve ve ve

Love

Be still, my soul: the Lord is on thy side.

ee

ee ee ee ee ee

ee ee ee ee ee

ee ee ee

ee ee ee

Seek

ee

ee ee ee ee ee

ee ee ee ee ee

ee ee ee

ee ee ee

Seek

Lord my God, you gave
me life and restored it
when I lost it.

St. Anselm

oo

oo oo oo oo oo

oo oo oo oo oo

oo oo oo

oo oo oo

Look

oo

oo oo oo oo oo

oo oo oo oo oo

oo oo oo

oo oo oo

Look

This is the plan determined for the whole world: this is the hand stretched out over all nations.

Isaiah 14:26

wr

wr wr wr wr wr

wr wr wr wr wr

wr wr wr

wr wr wr

unwrap

wr

wr *wr* *wr* *wr* *wr*

wr *wr* *wr* *wr* *wr*

wr *wr* *wr*

wr *wr* *wr*

Unwrap

All glory, laud, and
honor to you,
Redeemer, King

Palm Sunday

The Final Week

Lowercase b has both a counterclockwise and a clockwise stroke. The shift in directions is an opportunity for mistakes, unless you're prepared for it. Showcase your best transitions for a perfect letter b.

You'll close out Holy Week with the most common letter combinations.

Congratulations on making it this far! As we step into the most solemn days on the Church calendar, think about how you can use your new skills to bless others. Handlettering adds a personal touch to cards, gift tags, and thank-you notes.

be bo bu er ol it ai

be

be be be be be

be be be be be

be be be

be be be

Remember

be

be be be be be

be be be be be

be be be

be be be

Remember

O Lord, remove not thy help to a distance from me: look towards my defense.

bo

bo bo bo bo bo

bo bo bo bo bo

bo bo bo

bo bo bo

Labor

bo

bo bo bo bo bo

bo bo bo bo bo

bo bo bo

bo bo bo

Labor

Fear not. I am with thee.
O be not dismayed. For
I am thy God. and will
still give thee aid.

bu

bu bu bu bu bu

bu bu bu bu bu

bu bu bu

bu bu bu

Rebuke

bu

bu bu bu bu bu

bu bu bu bu bu

bu bu bu

bu bu bu

Rebuke

The LORD is my strength and my defense: he has become my salvation.

Exodus 15:2a

er

er er er er er

er er er er er

er er er

er er er

Wonder

er

er er er er er

er er er er er

er er er

er er er

Wonder

What wondrous love is this that caused the Lord of bliss to bear the dreadful curse for my soul, for my soul.

ol

ol ol ol ol ol

ol ol ol ol ol

ol ol ol

ol ol ol

Behold

ol

ol ol ol ol ol

ol ol ol ol ol

ol ol ol

ol ol ol

Behold

Behold the wood
of the Cross, whereon was
hung the Saviour of
the world.

it

it it it it it

it it it it it

it it it

it it it

Spirit

it

it it it it it

it it it it it

it it it

it it it

Spirit

Father, into your hands
I commend my spirit.

Luke 23:46

ai

ai ai ai ai ai

ai ai ai ai ai

ai ai ai

ai ai ai

Wait

ai

ai ai ai ai ai

ai ai ai ai ai

ai ai ai

ai ai ai

Wait

There is a great silence on earth today. a great silence and stillness. The whole earth keeps silence because the King is asleep.

St. Epiphanius

Easter Sunday

Christ is Risen

He is risen indeed. Happy Easter!

There's nothing new to learn or practice today, the highest feast day of the liturgical year.

Take a moment to appreciate the progress you've made. Look back to your first page. See how far you've come! Even after you finish this Lenten journey, keep practicing your new-found skills.

P.S.
Download the full-color Easter Octave pages, full of the joy of the risen Christ, at booksfaithlife.com/easter

Made in the USA
San Bernardino, CA
18 February 2020